OF BOUNDLESS DOMAINS

OF BOUNDLESS DOMAINS

BY MICHAEL I. SOVERN

photography by

DAVID FINN

FRED KNUBEL

with a foreword by

FRED W. FRIENDLY

UNIVERSITY PRESS OF AMERICA

"All that the human mind

can conceive,

all that the human heart

can feel—

these boundless domains

are ours to explore."

Designed by Ruder·Finn Design, Inc., NYC

Copyright © 1994 Michael Sovern
University Press of America®, Inc.
4720 Boston Way
Lanham, Maryland 20706

3 Henrietta Street
London WC2E 8LU England

Library of Congress Cataloging-in-Publication Data
Sovern, Michael I.
Of boundless domains/by Michael I. Sovern; photography by David
Finn, Fred Knubel: with a foreword by Fred W. Friendly.
p.   cm.
ISBN 0-8191-9627-4 (cloth: alk. paper)
1.Columbia University. 2. Higher Education--United States. I. Title.
LB2331.S66   1994
378.1'25--dc20   94-19526
                                                                   CIP

TABLE OF CONTENTS

F O R E W O R D

Twenty-eight years ago, soon after resigning as President of CBS News, I was told that Columbia University was considering me for a tenured professorship. Though I was truly honored by this academic prospect, I dreaded the possibilities of endless red tape and assessments of my qualifications. I said that I would be interested, but I would not hold still to be tested by some *ad hoc* committee of non-descript faculty members to investigate my academic credentials.

The President of Columbia, a predecessor of Michael Sovern, quickly reassured me that all he needed was a copy of my *curriculum vitae*. "It's yours," I said, "on one condition: that you tell me what *curriculum vitae* means."

My skills in Latin translation were sadly lacking, though my vocabulary of phrases has expanded slightly over the last quarter century or so. What I felt particularly challenging as I joined the Columbia faculty was the marvelous opportunity to explore thinking processes in a new setting and to help students think out issues.

I met Michael Sovern shortly after I arrived at Columbia; he and I would frequently talk about the shrinking opportunities for good reporting and good dialogue and our hopes for thoughtful exchanges in the classroom.

The spoken word is alive but not well. Political oratory, once aloft on the wings of Churchill, Roosevelt, Stevenson, and a hundred others, is largely confined to the twenty-second sound bite.

Network news, which owes its prestige to the in-depth reporting of Edward R. Murrow and his colleagues, has become a series of headlines. Even the Broadway theater, once home to dozens of dramas, is now more a haven for musicals.

Yet there is hope for good talk, much of it to be found on the American college campus. It is no coincidence that those lively Socratic dialogues that have engrossed PBS television audiences for the past seventeen years, an enterprise of the Columbia University Seminars on Media and Society, were based on Law School techniques that my colleagues and I had adapted for classes at the Columbia Graduate School of Journalism.

In a society increasingly addicted to mumbles and rap, the classroom is one of the last hold-outs. Professors in the best universities are still expected to inspire and students are still taught to communicate persuasively. I soon realized that the teacher's job was not to make up minds but to open minds and to make the agony of decision so intense you can escape only by thinking. To quote from Mike Sovern,

> *Classrooms are not pulpits. Universities do not exist to preach. But we do offer earnest exploration of difficult questions in a disciplined way. In the right hands that method works as well for ethics as it does for less exalted subjects. Aristotle understood that. So did Socrates.*

Being a journalist by nature, I learned that Michael Sovern had been a scholarship student at Columbia College, commuting by subway from his home in the South Bronx. He was graduated first in his class at Columbia Law School and, at age twenty-eight, became the youngest full professor in the modern history of the

University. It was not surprising that he then became Dean of the Law School, Provost of the University, and President of Columbia for thirteen years, from 1980 to 1993. I was privileged to serve under him, and with him.

As student, teacher, and academic leader, Mike has always had a great deal to say; some of it is in this book, excerpted from a few of the hundreds of speeches he delivered during his presidency of Columbia. Like all great educators, he raises the right questions; he does not pretend to know all the answers. Since we both believe in the power of reason and the complexity of ethical choices, I find that Mike and I are in agreement much of the time.

More important than what people think is that they do think —that they are "thinking reeds," to borrow from Rebecca West. Mike Sovern's thoughtful approach to life, his wit and his optimism shine through whether he is talking about Einstein or Columbia's Lou Gehrig, campaign financing or the future of our children, scientific illiteracy or our abysmal international ignorance, Tiananmen Square or the Second Law of Thermodynamics, the Ten Commandments or—a favorite topic of his and mine— the First Amendment.

The photographs of sculpture and architecture at Columbia University, taken by David Finn and Fred Knubel, join with Mike's words to create a collection of ideas and pictures worth pondering. They are food for thought in an era when thinking hard and often is the world's best hope.

—Fred W. Friendly

GREAT
TEACHING

Each year thousands of parents entrust colleges and universities with a central role in their children's lives — an act of faith nothing short of remarkable. To be worthy of that trust, we aspire to transmit the heritage of civilization; to unlock the treasures of the past; to bring fresh vision and new discipline to the ever-growing fund of human knowledge; to enliven curiosity; to cherish the freedom to explore and express; to encourage joy in the presence of beauty, appreciation in the sharing of wisdom, excitement in the quest of learning, and pride in the glory of achievement.

We try to impress upon our students the importance of answering a question as clearly and succinctly as possible. I wonder how many political careers we have destroyed aborning.

A dedicated teacher is the custodian of civilization. A good teacher passes that trust on in no worse state than it was found. The great teacher illuminates ideas to the point where the student is forever changed in looking at the world and in making an impact on the world.

There are great teachers who displace their subject matter: the folklore has it that those who studied with Thomas Reed Powell studied Thomas Reed Powell whatever the name of the course. And there are great teachers who enrich their subject matter: their performances are not an exaltation of self but, paradoxically, a subordination of self. They perform to help their students learn, not to imprint a vision of virtuosity.

College students today are embarking on a voyage of discovery, exploring new challenges, mastering new skills and, in the process, learning more about themselves. If I weren't having such a good time myself, I would envy them.

We are a community—a marvelously diverse, wonderfully creative community. We come from all 50 states and more than 100 countries. We worship different gods; the range of our skin colors would challenge the most gifted artist; some of us live with disabilities; we are male and female, heterosexual and homosexual, young and old; we disagree about many, many things. What a wonderful way to learn!

If the best are not attracted to the classroom podium, their places will be taken by the second-best, and that will define our aspirations and achievements into the next century. If ever there were a nationwide emergency, seen clearly in advance so that those in power could take action in time, it is the critical challenge posed by the need to encourage the development of high quality professors to carry on the education of America.

Columbia is many things, but to me she is above all the inspiration of great teacher-scholars, the excitement of eager students, and the discoveries, large and small, that flow from their work together.

I am a teacher. I believe, as anyone who devotes his life to helping others must believe, that nothing here on earth is more important than appreciating the value of one human being.

INTERNATIONAL LEARNING

How can we guard against the illusionary and the irrational in international relations? If we are to improve what America says and does in the world, we will need to develop more knowledge, deeper understanding, a willingness to face complexity rather than hide behind rhetorical shields, an ability to analyze information dispassionately, a fluency in the subtleties of more than our own language, an informed insight into the heritage and value systems of cultures far different from our own. We must start with the young if we are to have any hope of elevating America's international expertise to a level that will earn the respect of our adversaries, the trust of our allies, and the confidence of Americans.

We know that success among nations requires learning and prudence, difficult and intricate work — attributes that America does not always display to the world in abundance. But I do think we have the human resources for a vast improvement. I see them every day — the young men and women who will someday help determine how we as Americans conduct ourselves in the world. To the extent that we help them prepare, we will strengthen our international commerce, we will enhance our national security, and, above all, we will brighten the prospects for a realistic and enduring world peace.

It may be good realpolitik to talk of war as the continuation of diplomacy by other means, but another truth would simply brand war as the failure of diplomacy.

We must move toward a global vision of scientific effort and support. We must use international strategies as effectively for the meeting of minds as for the rattling of sabers.

As a nation, we tolerate ignorance of the world at our peril. As a university, we share an obligation to see that all the regions of the world are studied in depth, even those that don't make the evening news — until the next surprise.

Traditional course offerings in Western civilization are insufficient. They do not take account of the interdependence of cultures in the modern world; they miss the insights to be gained from comparative study; and they fail to make the most of the interests of many of our students, a far more diverse group than we have ever taught before. Yet a first-class program in Western civilization is a thing of beauty. We should not dilute it. We should complement it, extending the core to other civilizations, contemporary issues and contemporary thinkers.

Students should make contact with another culture in a way that translations can't convey.

If we learn more about others and come to understand them, perhaps we shall bring closer the day when we no longer define them as "others."

ETHICS

The key to great teaching and inspired learning is the unembarrassed acceptance of the responsibility to try to lead to the good.

We expect our graduates to be far more than skillful at their callings and prodigious in their earnings. We want lawyers with a passion for justice and business leaders who understand that the good bottom line, though indispensable, is insufficient by itself. We want all of our graduates to be able to take pride in a society they help to define, and in a free enterprise system of which social responsibility is an integral part.

Classrooms are not pulpits. Universities do not exist to preach. But we do offer earnest exploration of difficult questions in a disciplined way. In the right hands that method works as well for ethics as it does for less exalted subjects. Aristotle understood that. So did Socrates. And now and then a gifted teacher helps a student to sense the ineffable.

When the majesty of the Ten Commandments is lost in the thicket of regulations, we must prune away the underbrush.

An undertaking as large and diverse as higher education is not going to be as pure as the driven snow. Scientific fraud, irresponsible polemics, greed, avarice and other deadly sins are bound to afflict us. But we must not be tolerant of them. We are and wish to be the repositories of hopes and dreams, the means to improve our society. We must do all we can to be exemplars of integrity and decency.

As important as what students do and professors teach is what our institutions stand for. A university can design new courses in applied ethics, it can foster ethical discussion in its old courses, it can marshal its students in morally rewarding pursuits, but all this is to little avail unless the institution itself behaves ethically.

Truth seems obtainable, definitive. Goodness is elusive, debatable. To the disciplined academic, who has been trained not to profess what he does not know, to claim only what he can prove, silence is preferable to sermonizing. In an era in which confused voices impatiently cry for relevance, asking what is good may seem beside the point. But the passion for the good is still there among many, many young people. It is their elders who make cynics of them. Like martinis, cynicism is an acquired taste.

Education should instruct in the exercise of judgment, the making of choices, the awareness that the pursuit of one good commonly entails at least the partial sacrifice of another. But it should also lead the participants to conclude that some conduct cannot be rationalized. Some conduct is simply wrong.

❦

If we are to travel the long road together, a road of hard work and good faith, we cannot accept bigotry from any group toward any group.

❦

Every individual must be sacred to us. If we allow anyone or any group to ride roughshod over the rights of others, we abdicate our moral responsibility.

It has been observed that ours would be a far better country if more people obeyed just two of the Ten Commandments. Any two.

Improvement of our campaign financing laws is essential not only because the current system is both inequitable and fraught with dangers of corruption, but also because the erosion of trust in our political processes contributes to the general loss of faith in the integrity of government and creates a climate for other abuses.

I believe with my friend Will Gaylin that the most pressing ethical issue of our time is the rediscovery of community, that in the joy of our boundless freedom in America, we have lost the sense of sacrifice, of limits on our autonomy, of service to others.

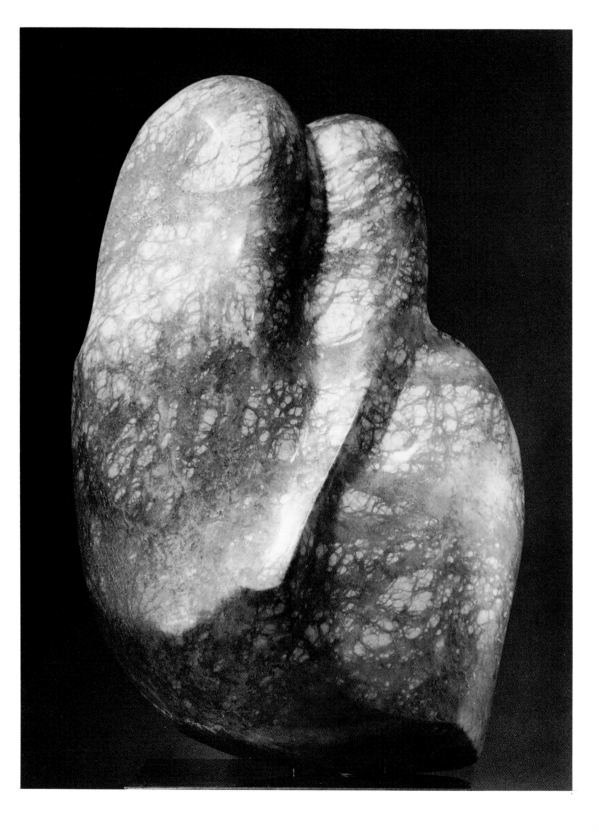

The capacity to find one's own happiness in the service of others is the greatest gift of life. You cannot cure all the ills of the world, but you can do far more than you may yet realize. The moral test of your life will not be what the world is like when you leave it, but whether you did your part, as best you could, to make this small and fragile planet a better place.

NATIONAL STRENGTH

We have in America almost twenty-six million people between the ages of eighteen and twenty-four. Properly educated, they can become an invincible army of productive workers, an informed citizenry capable of realizing democracy's dreams, a people able to make the most of life.

A great university needs the vision of enlightened government leaders; it needs the generosity of alumni who believe, rightly of course, that they got more than they paid for; and it needs the wisdom of the best in business who understand the importance of investing in human capital.

What is done in the next few years about preserving and strengthening the quality of education will say a great deal about whether we intend to invest wisely in our country's future. Those who study the past for clues to the future know with certainty that the investment in human capital on the American campus has brought a remarkable return in national strength and world leadership.

Without a healthy system of higher education, there cannot be an informed and cultivated citizenry; there cannot be a vibrant economy; there cannot be a strong America.

So much can be accomplished through Presidential leadership and commitment. A President who sets a positive tone on civil rights and opportunities for minorities and women will strengthen educational opportunity. A President who brings intellectuals, scholars, artists, scientists and teachers to the White House underscores their value to the nation. A President who is current on educational issues and makes frequent appearances on college campuses tells the nation and the world that he knows where the future lies.

A strong society preserves and enhances the best of its heritage even as it plans and builds for tomorrow.

There is no question that national action is required to serve our most vital national interest: the future of our children, which is, of course, the future of our nation. Our educational responsibility as a society begins long before school and even before birth. Prenatal care, nutrition, drug-free pregnancy are the beginnings of a continuum of development that will profoundly affect opportunity for success in high school, college, and graduate school.

Our system of higher education is that sector of our economy still acknowledged to be the best on earth. It even enjoys a favorable trade balance. It is currently educating more than thirteen million people. It employs more than two million, including a large percentage of the world's Nobel Prize winners. It spins off jobs for millions more; it annually attracts over a million foreigners to our shores; it pumps some $100 billion into our economy; it generates the fundamental ideas and prepares the people to keep us competitive in a high-technology world.

The key to national greatness lies in people, not in things. I hope

we will win an appeal to nobler instincts — to a deeply felt ideal that

those able enough to go on to the best colleges should be helped to

attend them. Those who do not share that ideal endanger our nation's

economic self-interest by wasting valuable human resources.

We live in a society where every candidate talks — and every parent nods approvingly — about protecting the future for our children. Are we serious? The future we are delivering to our children will be clouded by an obscene Federal deficit, higher taxes, a Social Security system they will support but which may well be unable to support them, skyrocketing costs of education and housing, an environment polluted by negligence and corner-cutting — and that is just the beginning of the future we are giving them. It is not just to the poor but to all children that we seem to be saying through our actions: "We are aboard; now we're going to pull up the ladder." Again and again our nation suffers because few politicians dare to risk stepping out years ahead of public awareness.

We cannot guarantee that every public servant will be honest, though surely most are. But we can make life more difficult for the crooks — by ordering the way government does its business to minimize opportunities for abuse, to make detection more likely and punishment more probable.

Though we in America struggle and stumble, we remain optimists at heart, enduring believers in the dream of equal opportunity on which our nation was founded, daring to hope that, ultimately, just as the world watched the awesome dawn of our government of the people, by the people, and for the people, so will we prove worthy to help others by our example find the way to a free and fair interracial society.

Einstein observed that our age is characterized by a perfection of means and a confusion of goals. Surely, we have within our grasp the means to confront the most pressing problems of poverty, health, education and discrimination, if we decide what kind of nation we are and what kind of world we seek.

FREEDOM OF EXPRESSION

We know that wherever tyranny takes hold, whether of the left or of the right, the first targets of oppression are the forums of education, communication, and the arts.

Journalistic criticism of our elected leaders is not always wise. The angry reports about those officials are not always fair. But I would far rather live in a country where the media and the government complain about each other than one in which harmony is enforced, dissent driven underground.

We at the University know that freedom for scholars and freedom for journalists is indivisible: the freedom to ask whatever questions they wish and to communicate whatever answers they find without fear of retribution, without clearance by censors. To keep alive and well the spirit of inquiry — that is our common cause.

Journalists and scholars share a profound concern about a public that swings wildly from admiration to distrust of the media. We must seek the causes of this inconstancy together, for the words of the First Amendment may be safe from a distrustful people, but its spirit is not.

Fashions come and go, and in the long course of human history, so does freedom of expression. Eternal vigilance — guarding always — is our central responsibility.

Complacency is an often subtle but always monstrous enemy of freedom. It is no friend to the champions of liberty abroad; it is no friend to our own democracy; and it is certainly no friend to endangered foreign students who deserve every possible act of friendship and protection.

Some would have us believe that freedom is humanity's destiny and that our destiny is at hand. I do believe that freedom is undying, that the idea of freedom is an idea as immortal as any mortals can conceive. Yet few activities appear so simple in passion and are so complex in fact as securing and upholding freedom. Let us maintain a healthy anxiety about the so-called "inexorable" road to freedom. There is nothing "inexorable" about it. The peaceful revolution in Wenceslas Square succeeded. The peaceful revolution in Tiananmen Square did not.

LIFE
AND LIVING

The difficulties of day-to-day life remind me of the question put by Charles DeGaulle when he answered the call in France. "How," he asked, "can anyone govern a nation that has 245 different kinds of cheese?"

Forget the past and forget the press. I get a bad story every now and then that makes me mad as hell. Then I ask myself: which story got me this mad a year ago? And I can't remember. Most of the news is written in sand.

I obviously do not like the idea that I have made mistakes. But I must live with them. Perfection is not the destiny of man. Even Babe Ruth struck out 1,330 times.

Life is difficult business under the best of circumstances. And the best of circumstances exist only in the past or in the future.

Anyone can make a mistake, though perhaps only a fool makes the same mistake twice. Don't stress people's mistakes. Work to build confidence, not to tear it down.

Yes, I know our football won-lost record. Like you, I'd rather win than lose. But defeat tests us in ways that victory never does.

We spend so much time on matters that are urgent that we have too little left to spend on those that are important.

Authority is not like a muscle. It does not have to be exercised frequently to be effective.

Anyone who believes that the world cannot be changed hasn't been reading the papers. We see ideas override reality every day.

Enjoy how far we've come, but please don't rest until New Year's Eve.

❧

I have no patience with those who, corrupting technology, look upon

our times as an age when everything is disposable, including people.

❧

Choose a road that will challenge you in your daily work so that

you continue to stretch and grow your whole life long.

IN SEARCH
OF TRUTH

All that the human mind can conceive, all that the human heart can feel — these boundless domains are ours to explore.

We in the universities should think of fundamental inquiry the way we think of art. The impulse to do it is not practical. The search for knowledge, for understanding, is an eternal quest, a powerful inspirational force. This above all else we must preserve and protect.

Our trust in the power of disciplined inquiry, and in the value of the search for rational approaches, is such that we can sustain our belief, despite all the bleak forecasts for the modern world, that the best in civilization will survive.

Like the attainment of perfection, the comfort of simplicity is not ours on this earth. A great university prides itself on the discomfort of complexity, the uncertain ends of skepticism, the unknown destinations of the search for truth. We shall never have all the answers, but we hope we have helped our students ask the right questions. So long as the spirit of free inquiry is alive, we shall be ever wary of those who claim absolute knowledge. In that sense, the university is an oasis in a desert of omniscience.

The truth can never be known once and for all. Fundamental inquiry is never finished. What we know is the beginning, not the end.

Many years have passed since C.P. Snow suggested that the humanist who cannot describe the Second Law of Thermodynamics is as illiterate as the scientist who has not read Shakespeare. We should get on with it.

We have yet to solve the problem of scientific literacy for the nonscientist. We pronounce a national scandal the inability of our young to recognize, much less to write, a clear sentence. But we tolerate with remarkable equanimity a similar inability to know what it means to think scientifically, to understand the processes by which our universe functions and to appreciate the difference in our lives that such knowledge makes. We pay for that ignorance with erratic swings between policies founded first on wonder and awe, then on fear and mistrust.

A great university can be likened to a great cathedral — an enduring expression of faith, a soaring commitment of the spirit. But a university is never finished. Each generation has its chance to put new stones in place as we reach toward the sky.

P L A T E S

Cover: "Alma Mater," 1901; Daniel Chester French; Low Memorial Library Steps.

Frontispiece: The Rotunda of Low Memorial Library, reflected in one of its marble columns.

Table of Contents: A column base at the entrance to Avery Hall.

Foreword: An Earl Hall globe light seen through the campus entrance gates at 117th Street.

Page xii: "Alexander Hamilton," 1908; William Ordway Partridge; Hamilton Hall Steps.

Page 2: "Life Force," 1992; David Bakalar; Charles H. Revson Plaza.

Page 7: "Three-Way Piece: Points," 1967; Henry Moore; Charles H. Revson Plaza.

Page 8: "Letters," 1916; Charles Keck; Broadway at 116th Street, Main Gate South.

Page 10: Interior, St. Paul's Chapel.

Page 12: Campus entrance gates, Broadway and 116th Street, winter.

Page 17: Carving over the entrance to Avery Hall.

Page 18: "The Great God Pan," 1899; George Gray Barnard; Lewisohn Lawn.

Page 20: "The Thinker," cast 1930; Auguste Rodin; Philosophy Lawn.

Page 24: Stairwell lamp in Low Memorial Library.

Page 26-27: "Three-Way Piece: Points," 1967; Henry Moore; Charles H. Revson Plaza.

Page 29: Side door of St. Paul's Chapel.

Page 30: "Alma Mater," 1901 [Back view]; Daniel Chester French; Low Memorial Library Steps.

Page 33: Lion relief near entrance to Butler Library.

Page 34: "Lovers II," 1975; Joan Sovern; Gray alabaster; Jerome L. Greene Hall.

Page 36: Exterior column of Low Memorial Library.

Page 39: "Bellerophon Taming Pegasus," 1967; Jacques Lipschitz; Jerome L. Greene Hall, West Facade.

Page 42: "Alma Mater," 1901 [relief]; Daniel Chester French; Low Memorial Library Steps.

Page 45: "Alma Mater," 1901; Daniel Chester French; Low Memorial Library Steps.

Page 46: "Thomas Jefferson"; William Ordway Partridge; Journalism.

Page 51: Volute of a column's capital in the Rotunda of Low Memorial Library.

Page 52: Detail, west wall of Schermerhorn Hall.

Page 56: "Scientia," 1925; Charles Keck Broadway at 116th Street, Main Gate North.

Page 59: "Le Marteleur," 1884; Constantin Meunier; Mudd Terrace.

Page 60: A stairwell of St. Paul's Chapel.

Page 62: "Le Marteleur," 1884; Constantin Meunier; Mudd Terrace.

Page 66-67: Interior, St. Paul's Chapel.

Page 68: "Alma Mater," 1901; Daniel Chester French; Low Memorial Library Steps.

Page 70: Exterior, St. Paul's Chapel.

Page 74: "The Curl," 1968; Clement Meadmore; Uris Hall Lawn.

Page 77: Exterior column bases, Low Memorial Library.

Page 78: Dome windows, St. Paul's Chapel.

Photo Credits:
David Finn: Cover, Pages: xii, 2, 7, 8, 18, 20, 26-27, 30, 34, 39, 42, 45, 46, 56, 59, 62, 68, 74.

Fred Knubel: Frontispiece, Table of Contents, Foreword, Pages: 10, 12, 17, 24, 29, 33, 36, 51, 52, 60, 66-67, 70, 77, 78.